THE ALCHEMY OF DREAMS

Deciphering the Mysteries of the Sleeping Mind to Unveil Their Profound Messages, Avert Impending Dangers and Transform Your Waking Life

By

Gerald M. Brannon

TABLE OF CONTENT

INTRODUCTION

With over 40 different dreams and their deep physical and spiritual interpretations, "The Alchemy of Dreams" reveals the profound secrets hidden inside your nighttime visions. This captivating guide leads you on a journey through the mysterious realm of dreams, uncovering their hidden messages, significance and providing practical methods to help you transform your waking life.

Gerald Brannon, an expert in dream analysis and psychology with years of expertise in both academic research and practical application, offers a thorough examination of the science, history, and spiritual components of dreams. The author's in-depth grasp of the subconscious mind, as well as his considerable experience with dreamers from all backgrounds, provide a unique viewpoint on this intriguing subject.

Inside "The Alchemy of Dreams," you will find:

The Science of Dreaming: Learn about the intricate mechanisms of sleep cycles and the brain's role in dream production.

The Various Types of Dreams: Explore the dream world's vast geography, from lucid and nightmares to recurring and prophetic dreams.

Dream Symbols and meanings: Interpret common dream symbols and personal patterns to learn what messages your subconscious is sending you.

Psychological and spiritual insights: Learn about dream interpretation ideas, as well as the spiritual meaning behind your dreams.

Enhanced Dream Recall: Improve your dream memory, practice lucid dreaming, and use your dreams for emotional healing and personal growth.

"The Alchemy of Dreams" is not just a book; it is a transforming experience. Whether you're an experienced dreamer or new to accessing your subconscious, this guide will help you use your dreams to unlock creativity, solve difficult problems, avert impending dangers and develop greater self-awareness.

Dreams have always fascinated the human mind, offering glimpses into our innermost longings, anxieties, and hidden thoughts. Throughout different cultures and time periods, dreams have held great importance, being seen as windows into the spiritual world, divine messages, or revelations about our deepest selves. When it comes to spirituality, dreams are commonly regarded as a connection between the physical and spiritual realms, allowing the soul to freely venture and discover beyond the limitations of the physical form. In numerous spiritual traditions, dreams are seen as a method of communication from higher powers or spiritual guides, providing guidance, warnings, or revelations to the dreamer.

From a scientific perspective, dreams are the result of intricate neurological processes that take place while we sleep. It is believed that they can be influenced by a range of factors, such as our thoughts, emotions, and experiences in our waking life.

Truth be told, dreams are how your body and mind find the right balance of power. Some dream symbols have general meanings that might not be clear at first glance. Most of the time, dream analysis tells you about a "possibility" of the future that you need to get ready for. It doesn't mean that everything you want, worry about, or fear will always come true. If you can figure out what your dreams mean, you can better understand yourself and make sense of things that seem strange or unlikely to happen. You need to pay attention to what they say and make good decisions when you're awake. Your job is to make good dreams come true and keep bad dreams from coming true.

CHAPTER ONE

Understanding the Mechanisms of Sleep Cycles

Sleep is a multifaceted and ever-changing phenomenon that is crucial for our overall physical and mental health. The process comprises multiple stages, each possessing distinct properties and fulfilling certain duties. This section explores the complexities of sleep cycles, encompassing:

The many stages of sleep, ranging from the less profound stages of light sleep (Stages 1 and 2) to the more profound stage of deep sleep (Stage 3) and the stage characterized by rapid eye movement (REM) sleep.

Sleep Architecture

Sleep architecture refers to the organization and structure of sleep, including the many stages and patterns that occur during a sleep cycle. The nocturnal progression of sleep encompasses multiple stages, each characterized by distinct physiological and neurological phenomena.

The human brain exhibits significant activity throughout sleep, particularly during REM sleep, which is associated with the occurrence of very vivid dreams. The neurobiology of dreaming examines the specific brain regions involved in the formation of dreams, such as the limbic system and the prefrontal cortex.

Neurotransmitters and hormones: They are responsible for the impact of chemical messengers such as serotonin, dopamine, and acetylcholine on the process of dreaming and sleep patterns.

Cerebral Electroencephalography: The cerebral electroencephalography comprehends the distinct brain wave patterns linked to different sleep stages and their correlation with the occurrence of dreams.

The cognitive mechanisms behind the brain's creative processes: Investigates the activation of the brain's creative and problem-solving faculties during dreams, which results in the emergence of innovative ideas and profound understandings.

The Phenomenon of Dreaming

The inquiry into the purpose of dreaming has captivated scientists, philosophers, and intellectuals for ages. There are a variety of theories that aim to elucidate the purpose of dreams:

Psychological Theories: This includes Sigmund Freud's view that dreams serve as a means to realize our wishes, and Carl Jung's belief that dreams provide insights into archetypes and the collective unconscious.

Cognitive theories, such as the activation-synthesis hypothesis and the continuity hypothesis, offer explanations for the nature of dreams. The activation-synthesis hypothesis proposes that dreams represent the brain's effort to interpret random neural activity. On the other hand, the continuity hypothesis implies that dreams mirror our conscious thoughts and worries.

Evolutionary theories investigate the concept that dreaming fulfills a purpose that helps an organism adapt, such as simulating threats or addressing problems.

Physiological Theories: Examining the impact of dreams on brain plasticity, the storage of memories, and the processing of emotions.

To get a comprehensive understanding of the deeper meanings and significance of your own dreams, it is essential to grasp the scientific aspects of sleep cycles, the brain's involvement in dreaming, and the diverse theories regarding the purpose of dreaming.

Exploring dreams and spirituality allows us to tap into the profound depths of our mind and soul. Both of them have the ability to uncover information that is not easily accessible to our conscious mind or logical reasoning. Both of these practices have the potential to deepen our self-awareness and provide guidance on our spiritual journey.

During our sleep, our minds conjure up a variety of scenarios, ranging from realistic to fantastical, often with recurring themes. However, the nature of dreams, their purpose, and their significance remain subjects of inquiry.

Dreams serve as a means for our subconscious and conscious minds to establish communication. They have the ability to assist us in understanding and managing our emotions, finding solutions to challenges, recovering from past traumas, tapping into our creative potential, and uncovering parts of ourselves that may have been hidden.

Dreams are a collection of visual scenes, feelings, ideas, and perceptions that manifest during our periods of sleep. These movements happen without control and usually take place during the rapid-eye movement (REM) phase of sleep. Dreams can occur at other points in the sleep cycle, but they are most vivid and memorable during REM. It is worth noting that not all individuals have the ability to recall their dreams. In fact, studies suggest that even those who do remember their dreams tend to forget approximately 95% of them upon awakening.

Analyzing your Dreams

Dream analysis has been recognized as valuable by many psychologists, particularly those who are involved in therapy. Therefore, dreams serve the purpose of organizing the information in our minds and also prompting us to contemplate information that we may overlook during our waking hours. During the day, our attention was directed towards tasks unrelated to the news regarding the presidential administration and endangered species. However, as we slept, our dreams allowed us to process our thoughts and emotions about this information.

Dreams can be seen as messages from the unconscious mind, if only they were expressed in the same language as our waking reality. Understanding dream symbols is crucial when it comes to interpreting dreams. Begin by keeping a dream journal and carefully noting down the characters, objects, places, events, and themes that seem particularly meaningful. Whenever a dream sign seems significant, it is crucial to explore it further.

Although there are universal definitions, dream analysis heavily depends on the dreamer providing a comprehensive explanation of their dream. When creating your records, pay close attention to the words you choose and the areas you emphasize in your retelling. These messages hold significant importance in the dream, as they have captured your attention, whether you were aware of it or not. By engaging in this process of self-awareness and reflection, you will establish a stronger connection with your inner self, who is ultimately the one who dreams your dreams.

Prior to delving into the underlying interpretations, it is essential to recall the precise details of the dream. Having a clear memory leads to a more precise interpretation.

Setting and Environment: Every dream has a backdrop, and the details of this backdrop can provide valuable insights. Regardless of whether it's a familiar place or an unknown territory, the environment can provide valuable insights into the essence of the dream.

Participants: Dreams frequently include a variety of characters, both familiar and unfamiliar. Identifying these individuals can provide valuable insights into the dynamics and emotions at play.

The essence of the dream is found in the unfolding events. By examining the actions, a more comprehensive understanding of the underlying themes and emotions can be obtained.

Objects and Elements: Some objects in dreams hold particular symbolic meanings. Understanding these factors can assist in deciphering the meaning of the dream.

Feelings experienced during the dream can offer insight into your current state of mind, serving as a reflection of your real-life emotions.

Recalling dreams

There is a significant variation in the ability of individuals to recall their dreams. While some individuals have a remarkable capacity to remember numerous dreams, others have a much more limited recollection. There is evidence to support the idea that biochemical factors may contribute to variations in dream recall. For those looking to enhance their dream recall, these techniques may prove helpful.

Before you drift off to sleep, make a mental note to yourself that you are determined to recall your dreams. Consider keeping a notebook and pen next to your bed to jot down your dreams. It is advisable to record any dreams that you may have during the night. Waiting until morning decreases the likelihood of remembering it. Upon waking up, it is beneficial to dedicate some time to recalling and documenting any dreams experienced during the night. It would be helpful to jot down any fragments you can recall. With time, you will gradually remember more and more specific details.

CHAPTER TWO

The Various Types of Dreams

Lucid Dream

A lucid dream is a dream in which the dreamer is aware and conscious. When in this state, one has the ability to exert self-control within a dream and embark on an exploration of an entirely novel realm. The level of control one can exert during lucid dreaming varies, but at the very least, you will be navigating through a realm created by your subconscious mind while fully conscious of the fact that you are in a dream. Lucid dreams are remarkable occurrences in which the dreamer attains consciousness of their dreaming state and frequently possesses the ability to manipulate the dream's storyline and surroundings.

In the majority of non-lucid dreams, individuals lack awareness of their dream state. An inherent feature of these dreams is that despite the occurrence of extremely peculiar events, they are perceived as genuine experiences. Only upon awakening do individuals come to the realization that what they experienced was really a dream. During a lucid dream, one is aware that the events occurring are not real and are actually happening within a dream. Frequently, this enables the dreamer to exercise a certain level of influence over the events taking place.

Lucid dreaming enables the dreamer to freely generate and construct any desired elements within the dream, making it a thrilling method to creatively and securely explore the boundaries of one's imagination while dreaming. Since the dreamer possesses a certain level of influence over the characters, settings, and occurrences within the dream, it serves as a means to encounter and investigate experiences that may be unattainable in one's ordinary existence.

There exist two distinct categories of lucid dreams:

Dream-initiated refers to the state in which you become aware of your consciousness while dreaming and recognize that you are in a dream.

Wake-initiated lucid dreaming involves transitioning directly from a state of wakefulness to a state of lucid dreaming. This variety is highly manageable and can be effectively anticipated with minimal effort.

Methods for Inducing a Lucid Dream

Enhance the duration of your Rapid Eye Movement (REM) sleep: It is advisable to augment the quantity of high-quality sleep obtained on a nightly basis. Enhance your sleep patterns by adhering to a regular sleep routine, refraining from using electronic devices prior to bedtime, abstaining from consuming large meals and caffeine in the evening, and ensuring a comfortable sleep environment.

Maintain a Dream Diary: Certain individuals have observed that keeping a dream diary increases the likelihood of experiencing lucid dreams. By prioritizing dreams, you can enhance your consciousness of the actual event.

Mnemonic Induction of Lucid Dreams (MILD): In this technique, you tell yourself repeatedly that you will dream and that you will be aware that you are dreaming. The approach depends on a sort of memory known as prospective memory, or the ability to remember future events, to activate a lucid dream state.

Practice Reality Testing: This technique entails completing checks while awake and asleep to detect if one is dreaming. For example, you might try pressing your finger against a wall to test whether you are dreaming. If you are not, the solid wall would stop your finger. In a dream, however, your finger might simply pass through the wall. Getting acclimated to completing reality testing while awake may assist make it easier to complete it when you are asleep.

Understanding Nightmares and Night Terrors

Nightmares are vivid dreams that can be quite distressing, usually happening during deep sleep. On the other hand, night terrors occur when someone is partially awake, leading to episodes of screaming, flailing, and visible signs of stress. While bad dreams or nightmares can happen from time to time, night terrors are infrequent and can be quite challenging. Nightmares and night terrors can be caused by factors such as anxiety, stress, or substance use during the day.

Sleep-related incidents known as night terrors can cause individuals to exhibit physical and verbal reactions as a result of distressing visions during their sleep. These occurrences take place during non-REM sleep stages and can prove to be quite challenging to awaken from. During a night terror, an individual may exhibit signs of extreme fear, accompanied by loud screams and vigorous movements while they are asleep. Night terrors are episodes during sleep that are considered undesired and fall under the category of parasomnia. Parasomnia is a sleep disorder characterized by atypical physical movements during sleep, like sleepwalking. The frequency and severity of parasomnia can vary significantly, resulting in disturbed and restless sleep for most individuals affected by this sleep disorder.

Nightmares are dreams that have a strong impact, feel very realistic, and cause distress, often abruptly waking you from sleep. Although bad dreams can contain unsettling content, nightmares abruptly awaken the sleeper. Upon waking, the dreamer may still experience feelings of anxiety and distress, accompanied by physical symptoms like a rapid heart rate or sweating.

Possible triggers and causes of night terrors can include:

Individuals who have gone through traumatic experiences may encounter nightmares and night terrors as a manifestation of post-traumatic stress disorder (PTSD). It is not uncommon for individuals to experience both PTSD and night terrors. In addition, it is worth noting that childhood trauma has the potential to give rise to night terrors, even in the absence of other symptoms commonly associated with PTSD.

Mood disorders such as depression, bipolar disorder, and generalized anxiety disorder have been found to be associated with the occurrence of nightmares. Although the relationship is not entirely evident, the added stress from these conditions might heighten the chances of having a night terror.

Factors such as stress, emotional distress, and heightened anxiety can contribute to the occurrence of night terrors.

Some medications, such as beta blockers, SSRIs, antihistamines, and certain sleep aids, have the potential to enhance the intensity and vividness of dreams, potentially leading to nightmares or night terrors.

Recreationally abusing drugs and alcohol can have a significant impact on the quality of sleep. Consequently, the individual will have a decrease in REM sleep and an increased likelihood of experiencing night terrors. In addition, night terrors commonly occur as a symptom for individuals experiencing alcohol withdrawal.

Patients with certain medical conditions, such as Parkinson's disease, may have a higher chance of experiencing nightmares and parasomnia, which can include night terrors and sleepwalking.

Individuals with a family history of recurring nightmares may have a genetic predisposition to experience night terrors.

Sleep disorders can disrupt the normal sleep processes and may lead to experiencing night terrors.

What Are the Causes of Nightmares?

Although the exact cause of nightmares is still uncertain, experiences during wakefulness can have a significant impact on the occurrence of nightmares. Dreams play a crucial role in the brain's processing of memories and emotions. Thus, nightmares can be seen as the brain's method of analyzing and dealing with trauma and fear. Causes of nightmares can range from everyday stressors to significant life changes.

- Various mental health conditions: Various mental health conditions can contribute to the occurrence of nightmares. These conditions encompass depression, anxiety, post-traumatic stress disorder (PTSD), and bipolar disorder.

- Some medical conditions, such as Parkinson's disease, heart disease, or cancer, can affect sleep patterns and make individuals more susceptible to experiencing nightmares.

- List of medications: Some medications, such as certain antidepressants, blood pressure medications, and beta-blockers, have been known to potentially cause nightmares.

- The effects of sleep deprivation: Disruptions in sleep patterns, such as irregular sleep or insomnia, can increase the chances of having nightmares.

There is a connection between sleep disorders, such as sleep apnea, and nightmares. Sleep disorders can disrupt the sleep cycle and result in lower quality sleep, which in turn may contribute to experiencing nightmares.

Recurring Dreams

Recurring dreams are those that repeat themselves with minimal variation in storyline or topic. These dreams can last days, months, or even years and can be positive or bad in character. Recurring dreams are subjective and, similar to other dreams, frequently filled with familiar faces. Recurring dreams can be identical each time or simply repeat the same scenarios or fears. Nevertheless, there are certain plotlines or themes that frequently appear in recurring dreams.

Certain themes tend to be more prevalent than others. For instance, the majority of individuals encounter recurring dreams involving the sensation of falling, whereas some individuals have recurring dreams about losing teeth. Recurring dreams that deviate from these themes or draw from personal experiences are not uncommon. Recurring dreams can vary in their level of clarity, ranging from vivid to somewhat elusive in our memory. Recurring dreams are not uncommon and can sometimes indicate underlying conditions such as post-traumatic stress disorder (PTSD) or generalized anxiety disorder (GAD). Individuals who encounter these disorders also exhibit other notable symptoms.

Individuals with PTSD often experience distinct recurring dreams compared to those who do not have this disorder. Revisiting the distressing events that triggered their PTSD is a frequent occurrence in their nightmares. Recurring dreams that evoke negative emotions can be quite distressing and challenging to cope with, even though they are a common occurrence during sleep for many individuals.

Other causes of recurring dreams include:

Unresolved issues:

Recurring dreams are generally the result of psychological stress or unresolved conflict. The subconscious mind processes unsolved issues or emotions through dreams.

Anxiety and Stress:

High amounts of stress and anxiety might cause repeated dreams. These dreams may represent the dreamer's current anxiety or worry.

Life Transitions:

Major life changes or transitions, like as moving, starting a new career, or ending a relationship, might cause recurring dreams while the mind analyzes these big occurrences.

Health Issues:

Some physical health conditions, such as sleep difficulties or certain drugs, can cause repeated dreams.

Recurring Dream Themes and Interpretations

Being Chased

Frequently indicates the avoidance of an issue or anxiety in daily life.

Falling:

Can signify a sense of uneasiness or lack of control.

Being unprepared for an examination or performance:

Indicates sentiments of inadequacy or fear of failure.

Losing teeth:

Frequently related with aesthetic concerns or a fear of aging.

Flying:

Can represent a desire for freedom or an escape from limitations.

Being trapped:

Shows feelings of being stuck in a circumstance or relationship.

Managing or Stopping Recurring Dreams

While repeated dreams may be a common occurrence during sleep for many individuals, those that elicit unpleasant feelings can be profoundly distressing and challenging to cope with. If you have concerns about your reoccurring dreams and they are causing sleep disturbances or interfering with your ability to handle everyday activities, consulting with your doctor can assist you in determining an appropriate treatment strategy.

Additionally, implementing lifestyle modifications can aid in managing or diminishing the frequency of your reoccurring dreams. The following items are included:

Therapy or counseling can help address recurring dreams, which are linked to many mental health disorders, including stress, frustration, and post-traumatic stress disorder (PTSD). Therapy and counseling, especially cognitive behavioral therapy (CBT), can be beneficial in these situations, specifically for addressing stress, post-traumatic stress disorder (PTSD), and nightmares.

Regular exercise enhances emotional resilience and facilitates the management of stressful situations. Regular exercise has been found to enhance both the quality and length of sleep.

Methods for achieving a state of relaxation: Relaxation activities such as breathing exercises, meditation, and guided visualizations have demonstrated efficacy in reducing stress. These activities can also be incorporated into your regular sleep routine.

When discussing your dreams, it has been found that engaging in therapeutic dream interpretation sessions may help decrease the frequency of reoccurring dreams.

Practicing excellent sleep hygiene, such as establishing healthy sleep habits and following a calming evening routine, can help improve your ability to sleep well, even if you are experiencing repeated dreams. Inadequate sleep can exacerbate feelings of anxiety and tension, therefore, prioritizing efforts to enhance the quality of your sleep can also have a positive impact on your emotional state.

Prophetic Dreams

Prophetic dreams are a category of dreams that certain individuals believe have the ability to foretell future occurrences or unveil truths about the current or past situations. These dreams are commonly regarded as having a profound, perhaps otherworldly, nature and are believed to be communications from a divine being, the subconscious, or other metaphysical origins. Their inexplicable ability to offer insights outside the realm of our conscious perception sets prophetic dreams apart from other types of dreams. They surpass the limitations of time and space, enabling us to observe events before to their actual happening in our conscious state. These dreams may signify individual experiences or maybe have a wider influence on society.

Prophetic visions can have a significant impact on an individual. These intense experiences often have a strong impact, eliciting strong emotions and deeply affecting one's subconscious mind. It is typical for visionaries to experience anxiety or heightened awareness upon awakening, as if they had been given a brief glimpse of an alternate reality.

The captivating nature of prophetic dreams is in their capacity to offer foresight into forthcoming events and offer advice in navigating the complexities of life. Many people assert that they have experienced premonitions or forewarnings in their visions, which have enabled them to make well-informed choices or take necessary safeguards.

Although individuals' prophetic dreams vary, there are certain shared elements that seem to be universal. During prophetic dreams, individuals frequently experience vivid and lifelike scenarios, often feeling fully immersed in the unfolding events. Some individuals report experiencing intense emotions such as dread or exhilaration during these dreams. Upon awakening after a prophetic dream, one frequently experiences a sense of déjà vu. This uncanny sense of recognition can lead individuals to question whether their dream provided them with a peek of events that will occur in the future.

In addition to these elements, symbols and metaphors also significantly contribute to predictive dreams. During the dreaming process, individuals frequently see visions or encounters that hold significant personal significance or symbolize broader concepts that hold importance in their life. To decipher the meaning of these images, engage in introspection and gain a deep understanding of your subconscious cognitive processes. It is crucial to bear in mind that not all dreams possess prophetic significance. Many of them just reflect our daily actions and thoughts. However, individuals who experience prophetic dreams may find them to be both peculiar and awe-inspiring. By analyzing the meaning of these dreams, we might gain valuable insights about our own selves and potentially enhance our decision-making abilities.

Amidst a tumultuous and bewildering environment, prophetic dreams offer us lucidity, assurance, and direction. They are undeniably a divine blessing, as they ignite our enthusiasm for thrilling possibilities, caution us about impending calamities, or guide us towards transformative revelations.

If you possess the ability to have prophetic dreams, it might be beneficial for you to keep a dream notebook within easy reach. It is impossible to predict the dream-like occurrences that may occur in your life, whether it be years, months, or even days from now.

Understanding Daydreams

Daydreams are a captivating and intriguing type of spontaneous, imaginative thinking that happens while we are conscious. Daydreams occur during periods of wakefulness, typically when our minds are relaxed and not occupied with immediate tasks, in contrast to dreams that happen during sleep. This section delves into the different facets of daydreaming. Daydreams are a sequence of thoughts, images, or fantasies that arise spontaneously in the mind during waking hours. They frequently incorporate situations that are detached from the present reality.

Daydreaming is linked to the activation of the default mode network (DMN) in the brain. This network is most active during periods of brain inactivity and when attention is not directed towards external stimuli. Daydreams come in different forms, varying from brief, passing thoughts to intricate, vivid fantasies. Common themes often involve wishful thinking, reflecting on past experiences, and envisioning future scenarios.

Advantages of Daydreaming

Enhanced Creativity: Daydreaming has the potential to stimulate creative thinking by providing the mind with the freedom to delve into various possibilities and ideas, unconstrained by the limitations of the real world. Daydreams have been a source of inspiration for numerous remarkable inventions and artistic creations.

Problem-Solving: Daydreaming can be a valuable tool for tackling complex issues and exploring different solutions. It allows for a mental space to think through problems and come up with innovative ideas. It encourages a thoughtful approach and can result in surprising revelations.

Daydreaming can serve as a way to mentally escape and find relief from stress and anxiety. It enables individuals to imagine favorable results and practice coping strategies for real-life obstacles.

Self-Reflection: Daydreaming allows individuals to delve into their inner thoughts, contemplating their aspirations, anxieties, and objectives. Engaging in this reflective process can result in a deeper understanding of oneself and foster personal development.

Addressing Excessive Daydreaming

Remaining focused: Although allowing oneself to daydream can have its advantages, excessive daydreaming can disrupt one's daily routine and hinder productivity. Practicing mindfulness and establishing dedicated periods for concentrated thought can assist in achieving a sense of equilibrium.

Productive Daydreaming: Encourage structured daydreaming sessions where you intentionally let your mind wander to generate ideas or solve problems. This can be a productive way to tap into your creativity and find innovative solutions. By incorporating daydreaming into your routine, you can enhance productivity.

Identifying Patterns: Take note of the times and reasons behind your daydreaming. Gaining insight into the triggers and patterns can assist in utilizing the beneficial aspects of daydreaming while mitigating any potential drawbacks.

Through a comprehensive understanding of daydreams, one can develop a deeper appreciation for this distinct cognitive phenomenon and harness its potential to foster creativity, problem-solving abilities, and emotional well-being. Engaging in deep reflection and imaginative thinking can be a valuable asset in enhancing various aspects of your life, both personally and professionally.

CHAPTER THREE

Common Dream Symbols and Their Interpretations

Interpreting symbols in dreams can offer valuable insights into the depths of our subconscious. The most prevalent dream symbols and their corresponding interpretations are listed below.

Water: Water symbolizes emotions, the subconscious mind, and the continuous movement of life. Still water often represents a sense of serenity and calmness, while chaotic water can suggest a state of emotional unrest or tension.

Flying: Flying is commonly associated with notions of freedom, ambition, and a strong drive to overcome obstacles. It can also convey a sense of control and empowerment in one's life.

Teeth Falling Out: Often linked to emotions of insecurity, apprehension about getting older, or worries about one's looks and self-perception.

Chase: Being pursued in a dream might suggest feelings of unease or a tendency to avoid certain situations in reality. It suggests a sense of being chased by a challenge or anxiety that requires addressing.

Death: Death in dreams is not always a negative symbol. It can actually represent transformation, the conclusion of one phase, and the commencement of another. It is often associated with important changes or the release of old habits.

Animals: Each animal holds its own unique significance. As an example, snakes may symbolize hidden fears or transformation, while birds can represent aspirations and freedom.

House: The house symbolizes the individual and the various facets of their character. Certain rooms can hold distinct symbolism, like the basement symbolizing concealed emotions or the attic embodying deeper thoughts and memories.

Although common symbols can provide general insights, personal symbols are distinct to each person and carry significant meaning based on personal experiences and emotions.

Personal Symbols and Their Significance:

Connections and Feelings: Examine the emotions and associations linked to personal symbols. Take a moment to reflect on how these emotions connect to your everyday experiences and present circumstances.

Contextual Meaning: The meaning of personal symbols can vary based on the specific context of the dream. Take into account the broader storyline and how the symbol aligns with it.

Symbol Evolution: Personal symbols have the potential to transform as your life experiences shape and mold them. Consistently examining and reevaluating these symbols can provide new perspectives and comprehension.

Exploring Archetypes in Dreams

Archetypes are universal, symbolic images that stem from the collective unconscious, a concept pioneered by Carl Jung. These symbols have a universal presence and hold significant meaning in the human mind.

The Hero symbolizes the aspect of oneself that is driven to conquer challenges and accomplish objectives. Dreams that include a hero often suggest a process of personal development and exploration.

The Shadow: Represents the deeper facets of your personality that you might be suppressing or disregarding. Encountering the shadow in dreams can prompt you to confront and integrate these aspects of yourself.

The Anima/Animus: The anima embodies the feminine aspects within a man, while the animus embodies the masculine aspects within a woman. These figures indicate a pursuit of equilibrium and the harmonious blending of qualities from both genders.

The Wise Old Man/Woman: Represents deep wisdom, valuable guidance, and profound insight. Dreams with this archetype may indicate a connection to your inner guidance or a desire for advice and support.

The Trickster embodies a sense of disorder, disturbance, and the defiance of conventions. The trickster has the ability to challenge your perceptions and prompt you to view things from a different perspective.

The Mother embodies qualities of nurturing, care, and creation. The mother archetype can suggest a necessity for self-care, or it might mirror your connection with your own mother or maternal figures in your life.

By gaining a comprehensive understanding of common dream symbols, personal symbols, and archetypes, one can delve into the profound meanings concealed within their dreams. By acquiring this knowledge, you can obtain valuable insights into your subconscious mind, enabling you to navigate your waking life with enhanced awareness and clarity.

Psychological Perspectives of Dreams

❖ **Examining Freud's Theories on Dream Interpretation**

Sigmund Freud, a pioneer in the field of psychoanalysis, made substantial contributions to our comprehension of dreams. His theories center on the concept that dreams reflect our innermost longings and fears, often stemming from childhood events and the subconscious.

• Dream Analysis: Freud's groundbreaking work, published in 1900, established the bedrock for contemporary dream analysis. He suggested that dreams serve as a direct pathway to the unconscious mind.

• Distinguishing between Manifest and Latent Content: Freud made a distinction between the manifest content, which refers to the actual storyline of the dream, and the latent content, which represents the hidden psychological meaning. He held the belief that the latent content unveils our genuine, unconscious desires.

• Dream Work: The process through which the unconscious mind transforms latent content into manifest content, often utilizing mechanisms like condensation, displacement, and symbolization.

• Freud proposed that dreams frequently mirror suppressed desires associated with the Oedipus complex. According to this theory, children unconsciously develop sexual desires for their opposite-sex parent and experience feelings of competition with their same-sex parent.

• Realizing Desires: In the heart of Freud's theory lies the concept that dreams symbolize the realization of desires that cannot be fulfilled in our conscious state, often due to societal taboos or suppressed emotions.

❖ Exploring Jung's Contributions to Dream Analysis

Carl Jung, a contemporary of Freud, took a different approach than Freud's focus on sexual and aggressive drives, presenting a more expansive perspective of the unconscious. Jung's theories bring a deep understanding of the collective unconscious and archetypes, which greatly enhance the study of dream analysis.

• The Collective Unconscious: Jung proposed the existence of a profound, collective layer of the unconscious that underlies the personal unconscious. This layer is believed to encompass universal experiences and archetypes.

• Archetypes: Universal, symbolic images that manifest in dreams and other forms of human expression, such as the Hero, the Shadow, the Anima/Animus, and the Wise Old Man/Woman.

• Individuation: The process of developing self-awareness and seeking harmony and wholeness within the mind. Jung emphasized the significance of dreams in the process of self-discovery and individual development.

❖ **Contemporary Psychological Approaches**

Modern psychology has expanded upon the work of Freud and Jung, integrating fresh theories and approaches to better comprehend dreams.

• Cognitive Theories: According to the activation-synthesis hypothesis, dreams are the brain's way of interpreting random neural activity. The continuity hypothesis proposes that dreams are a reflection of our concerns and experiences in our waking life.

• Neurobiological Perspectives: Recent advancements in neuroscience have shed light on the intricate workings of the brain during sleep, particularly emphasizing the significance of REM sleep in the occurrence of dreams and the contribution of the limbic system in the processing of emotions.

• Different Approaches to Therapy: Modern therapies, like cognitive-behavioral therapy (CBT) and Gestalt therapy, utilize dream analysis to uncover unconscious thoughts and emotions, aiding individuals in addressing psychological concerns and attaining personal development.

Interpreting Dreams as Spiritual Messages

Throughout history, dreams have been seen as a way to connect with the divine or spiritual realms.

• Historical and Cultural Beliefs: Exploring the different ways that cultures and religions have interpreted dreams as messages from higher powers, ancestors, or spiritual entities.

• Various Categories of Spiritual Dreams: Visions, prophetic dreams, and guidance dreams that offer valuable insights or warnings regarding future events or spiritual truths.

• Interpreting Spiritual Dreams: Methods for understanding the spiritual significance of dreams, such as meditation, prayer, and seeking guidance from spiritual mentors or guides.

Exploring Astral Projection and Out-of-Body Experiences

Certain dream experiences transcend the usual storytelling and delve into the realm of astral projection and out-of-body experiences (OBEs):

• Gaining Insight into Astral Projection: There is a belief that the consciousness has the potential to transcend the physical body and explore the astral plane, encountering various dimensions and realities.

• Techniques for Astral Projection: Utilize various methods like visualization, relaxation, and lucid dreaming to facilitate astral projection and explore realms beyond our own.

- Understanding and integrating OBEs: Exploring the interpretation of these experiences within your spiritual practice and personal growth.

Exploring Dreams and the Afterlife

Dreams can offer insights into the afterlife and facilitate connections with departed loved ones.

- Visitation Dreams: Dreams where deceased relatives or friends make appearances, often conveying messages of comfort, guidance, or unresolved matters.

- Exploring the Afterlife: Examining the significance of dreams in understanding beliefs about what happens after death, including concepts of reincarnation and the soul's journey beyond life.

- Exploring Afterlife Insights: Utilizing dreams to acquire a more profound comprehension of death, the afterlife, and the continuity of consciousness.

When examining dreams from both a psychological and spiritual perspective, one can gain deep understanding of our inner realms and the enigmas of life.

CHAPTER FOUR

Exploring the Deep Meaning of Dreams

- ### Feeling Trapped in a Particular Location

When one dreams of being trapped, it often signifies a concern about one's present circumstances. This could refer to various aspects of your life, such as your occupation, your personal connections, or even your geographical location. Your thought process often presents information in a nuanced manner. For instance, if you have concerns about your job impeding your ability to travel, your mind might manifest a dream where you feel confined. A dream involving feeling confined in a limited area typically indicates a sense of dissatisfaction with one's current circumstances and a desire for change. It is important to exercise caution when encountering dreams about being trapped, as they typically do not have positive connotations.

- **Dreaming About Babies**

This is a frequently occurring dream, and its interpretation is straightforward. Dreaming about babies typically signifies a desire to expand your family and leave a lasting impact for future generations. You aspire to be a parental figure in your children's lives and have a strong desire to improve the world. On the flip side of this dream, it's possible that you're not fully expressing yourself. Considering the possibility of children in your dreams may also indicate a desire to nurture and cultivate a deeper connection with your own inner child. It is often believed that there exists a hidden part within every individual, yearning to break free and express itself. Occasionally, this can be observed through the occurrence of dreams.

- **Dreams About water**

Dreams involving water may indicate a sense of being inundated or lacking support from your close ones. A dream involving water can have multiple interpretations, but its primary symbolism revolves around feelings of confinement or liberation. The interpretation is contingent upon the associations you make between water and your daily experiences. If a substantial quantity of water is present, it may indicate profound emotions or a powerful emotional response to a current event in your life.

- **Automobiles (specifically cars or vans)**

Dreaming about a vehicle typically lacks specific significance. However, if you dream about a car wreck or accident, it indicates a lack of confidence. It is imperative to give greater consideration to this particular form of dream, as it signifies emotional strain or a negative psychological condition. Dreaming about a car crash may signify concerns around potential losses, such as a job, relationship, or even one's residence. It is important to identify the root cause of these worries.

- **Dreams of teeth falling**

The dream of teeth falling out is a prevalent occurrence among individuals. Most individuals have experienced a dream where their teeth unexpectedly dislodge at some stage in their existence, and likely pondered over its significance. It appears that this dream is quite prevalent because when we are young and experience the loss of our first set of teeth (known as milk teeth), we feel afraid.

Therefore, it is unsurprising that the brain associates this initial encounter with dread and trauma with other situations in life that elicit feelings of anxiety or unease. Therefore, if you experience a dream where your teeth are coming out as an adult, it simply indicates that you are feeling fearful or anxious about the current transitions occurring in your life.

- **Dreams About Animals**

Interpreting this dream is challenging due to the fact that dreaming about a particular animal typically carries a different meaning than dreaming about animals in general. The majority of individuals experience dreams with animals at least once in their lifetime, typically occurring with greater frequency. Typically, a dream involving animals symbolizes a certain facet of your own personality or identity. Animals can be readily associated with specific personality traits or emotions. For instance, a snake could be linked to someone who exhibits deceitfulness or dishonesty.

A lion is often associated with individuals who possess strength, bravery, and great power. Interpreting dreams concerning a particular animal is typically quite straightforward. Occasionally, the animals that appear in our dreams may symbolize our contemplation of our own actions in reality.

- **Pursued by an entity**

Engaging in a hasty retreat or being pursued indicates a conscious effort to evade a source of distress or apprehension in one's waking existence. When contemplating the symbolic significance of being pursued, it may suggest that something is desiring to overtake you.

It is frequently associated with one's emotional response to a challenging aspect of their life that they are neglecting, such as an unacknowledged trauma or traumatic incident. During the dream, exerting effort to run faster by using your leg muscles actually hinders your progress, similar to attempting to fly. This situation is intriguing because it is possible that you have been exposed to an excessive number of horror films, leading to a fear of being pursued by someone. Pursuit sequences are frequently encountered in horror movies, and you may find yourself experiencing a sense of déjà vu as a result of recently watching a film. Alternatively, it can indicate that you are concerned about a matter that you have yet to address.

- **Examination Writing**

Have you ever experienced a dream in which you were undergoing an examination? These dreams could be the most frightening. The occurrence of feeling ill-equipped for an examination in a dream is frequently associated with the heightened strain and stress experienced by young adults or youngsters. It is a prevalent aspiration that numerous individuals encounter, and it can induce feelings of anxiety and worry even upon awakening. Dreams involving tests frequently symbolize self-assessment and contemplation. The exam serves as an assessment or trial that you encounter in your conscious existence, and your proficiency on the exam mirrors your perception of your competence in that particular domain. The nightmares of many individuals regarding tests might also be linked to their apprehension of failure and unease. Furthermore, these dreams may also reflect underlying concerns about inadequacy or falling short of expectations. Depending on the circumstances, it can signify the presence of a chance for advancement, acknowledgment, or affirmation, or it can indicate a concern about the possibility of not succeeding, being evaluated negatively, or being turned down. Exam dreams can also represent your aspiration for knowledge or validation, as well as your apprehension about meeting standards or confronting obstacles.

- **Nudity**

Have you ever experienced a dream that was uncomfortable, when you find yourself arriving at your employment or school completely naked? Alternatively, you might find yourself strolling along the street and suddenly become aware of your lack of clothing, or the fact that you have forgotten to wear your shirt or pants. Experiencing dreams when one is unclothed in a public setting can evoke intense feelings of embarrassment, humiliation, and vulnerability. These nightmares may indicate a sense of vulnerability or fear that others can perceive your true self behind the surface.

It may also indicate that you have difficulty in discovering your true identity or believe that you are being unjustly revealed or blamed. This particular dream is commonly associated with feelings of worry or vulnerability. It may occur when you have recently taken on a promotion, begun a new career, or are becoming more visible in public. However, an alternative perspective is that you possess a sense of ease with yourself and lack any hidden motives, indicating that you possess the self-assurance to openly present your true self to the world. And with whom you and others associate, as you understand that everyone is unique.

It can also symbolize a feeling of liberation, a longing for acknowledgement, carnal instincts, or a yearning for closeness and companionship. In certain public contexts, dreams involving nudity can be indicative of underlying feelings of anxiety, shame, or a fear of being judged or rejected by others. Consider the dream characters, the setting, and the emotions you experienced during the dream to identify the context.

- **Dreams About Death**

Dreaming of a loved one's demise or even your own demise can be an immensely distressing experience. However, it is important to note that such dreams do not necessarily indicate a nightmarish scenario or foreshadow an actual death. On the contrary, this dream motivates individuals to pursue a new venture or begin anew. These dreams may indicate a sense of unease regarding potential changes or uncertainties. Change can be intimidating as it brings uncertainty about what lies beyond. The mind often associates change with the unknown, much like the fear of death.

Thus, dreaming about the death of a loved one can indicate a fear of change, especially when it comes to children reaching significant milestones. The changes may suggest that a child is maturing and advancing in age, prompting a parent to ponder the whereabouts of their younger child. Therefore, dreams about dying can be seen as a way of grieving for the inevitable passing of time.

- **Dreams About Being Late**

This indicates a sense of concern and unease regarding the prospect of embarking on a new path in your life. You may have a strong sense of certainty regarding your ability to make a change. It may also indicate a sense of urgency to complete a task that you have been intending to do. Nevertheless, it seems that your subconscious is conveying the message that there is always an opportunity to attain your desires, regardless of the timing.

- **Dream About Clothing**

A dream about clothing often reflects your desire to present yourself in a certain way to others. Our clothes serve as a reflection of our identity and a means of self-expression.

For individuals who opt for vibrant and eye-catching colors, their choice of attire conveys a distinct message compared to someone donning a plain and unremarkable grey shirt. Wearing different clothes in your waking life compared to your dreams means that you may not be fully expressing your authentic self to others. If the dream symbol is shabby clothing, it might indicate feelings of unattractiveness or exhaustion. The color, style, and condition of the clothes can communicate various messages, reflecting aspects like self-assurance, individuality, social standing, or even the desire to conceal one's true self. For instance, if you consistently wear vibrant clothing in your dreams, despite not doing so in your waking life, it suggests that your mind is urging you to embrace self-expression and boost your confidence.

- **Dreaming of crosses**

Dreams that feature crosses can symbolize a range of spiritual, religious, or cultural beliefs. Depending on one's personal associations, crosses can symbolize hope, redemption, or sacrifice, as well as guilt, fear, or confusion. Crosses can also manifest in dreams as a representation of safeguarding or direction, particularly when circumstances in reality are ambiguous or disordered.

- **Dreams about a faulty Car**

During dreaming, certain regions of the brain become inactive, including those responsible for logical reasoning and language processing. There is a logical explanation for why mechanical and electrical objects tend to malfunction in dreams, or why reading becomes unexpectedly challenging. Using a smartphone, telling the time, or applying car brakes requires a clear state of mind. Symbolically, though, malfunctioning machinery can symbolize challenges or setbacks, along with feelings of frustration regarding one's performance.

- **Demons in Dreams**

Demons are cunning malevolent beings that personify fear, guilt, or negative impulses. These ominous entities could symbolize internal conflicts and unresolved emotions, possibly indicating a hidden desire to address negative behaviors. In different contexts, demons can represent various concepts such as suppressed desires, traumatic experiences, addiction, or even a spiritual struggle.

- **Food in Dreams**

Certain types of dream food can represent different emotions such as pleasure, indulgence, guilt, or excess. Various foods can reveal insights about your connection with your body, feelings of contentment or lack thereof, and your approach to generosity and hosting. Food can be seen as a symbol of knowledge, as it provides nourishment to the body, similar to how information nourishes the brain. However, at times, it could simply be food - a prevalent aspect of our daily routines that appears in dreams due to its frequency in our waking lives.

- **Dreams about houses**

When dreaming, houses or buildings are commonly linked to the inner psyche. Rooms or floors can serve as symbols for various emotions and interpretations of significant events. For example, a room can be either cluttered and chaotic or clean and organized. What is the ambiance of the house? Is it quiet, bustling, or somewhere in between? Each part of the house carries a unique atmosphere that reflects different periods in your life, your overall perspective on life, or various aspects of your inner being. From a more analytical perspective, houses can serve as a reflection of one's feelings of safety, comfort, and belonging. They can also indicate a desire for either change or stability.

- **Marriage in Dreams**

Marriage in dreams can signify a genuine longing for union or symbolize the integration of both feminine and masculine aspects of one's psyche. Marriage in dreams often represents a deep sense of commitment, the coming together of two individuals, and the alignment of their identities and aspirations. For some individuals, marriage dreams may be indicative of feelings of unease, doubt, or the desire to fit into societal or cultural standards. Take into account the context, your personal beliefs about marriage, and any other dream symbols to gain further insight.

- **Dreams about Killing Somebody**

When someone dreams of causing harm to another person, it does not imply that they have violent tendencies. Rather, it may symbolize their subconscious wish to eliminate certain aspects of their own character. The significance of the person you kill in your dream can reveal a lot about their character. Were they virtuous or malevolent? Murder can also represent a range of emotions and motivations, such as anger, frustration, revenge, fear, guilt, or the desire to gain control over a situation in reality. If you're experiencing recurring violent dreams, it is advisable to seek professional assistance.

- **Dreams about Flames**

Interpretations of dreams involving fire often suggest intense emotions and a strong sense of ambition, potentially indicating that you are fully engaged and motivated. Do you feel a passionate flame deep inside? Perhaps the dream fire symbolizes an unfulfilled passion or longing? When fires burn uncontrollably in a dream, it may indicate a challenge in managing intense emotions. On the other hand, the dreamer's visions of being near a fireplace could symbolize a sense of safety and comfort in their life. Does the fire in the dream represent a destructive adversary or a comforting source of warmth?

If you're engaging in risky behavior in a certain aspect of your life, it may be wise to heed the cautionary message from your dreams and carefully evaluate the potential outcomes. Fires have the potential to cause immense destruction and chaos. Nevertheless, following the fires, the bush undergoes a process of replenishment and transformation. Fire dreams may suggest possibilities for personal growth after experiencing emotional turmoil.

- **Missing a flight in a dream**

It is a commonly observed dream symbol where one misses a flight or any scheduled transport. This symbol often reflects the fear and frustration associated with missed opportunities in life. It is often experienced when faced with a significant decision or when one feels they are falling short of important objectives. In a dream, the act of missing a flight may indicate concerns about being left behind or abandoned by someone in your waking life.

- **Dreams about Fog**

Foggy dreams are quite common. Have you ever experienced the sensation of driving and suddenly encountering a thick fog that obscures the road ahead? Or perhaps you find yourself walking and struggling to navigate through the fog? The presence of dream fog suggests a certain opacity in regards to what lies ahead. At times, our dreams may reflect our state of emotional confusion. A state of emotional fog refers to a sense of confusion and a lack of clarity. It is possible that experiencing dream fog indicates a potential impairment in one's cognitive or visual clarity. At times, depression is depicted as a foggy presence.

Fog is intriguing and this fog could symbolize an enigma unraveling in your life.

- **Dreams about mountains**

In the realm of dreams, mountains often symbolize various hurdles, difficulties, or chances for personal development. Ascending a mountain can symbolize the pursuit of an objective, the craving for excitement, or the necessity to conquer challenges or apprehensions. If you reach the summit of your dream mountain, you must be feeling quite assured about life. Meanwhile, observing a mountain from afar, or witnessing the world from its summit, can evoke a sense of insight, understanding, or wonder about the entirety of your life.

- **Dreams about money**

Money dreams can represent various aspects of your life, such as self-esteem, relationships, and financial stability. They may also reflect your desire for success and material possessions. Money in dreams can be interpreted as a manifestation of various emotions, such as anxiety, greed, or a fear of poverty. If you dream of exchanging money, it could indicate that you are expecting significant changes in your life. In different situations, dreams involving money can also indicate a longing for financial autonomy, individual liberty, or acknowledgment.

- **Dreams about Schools**

If you're not currently attending school, a dream about school can symbolize the pursuit of knowledge, personal progress, and self-improvement. You may be considering the acquisition of new skills or training, along with the necessary socialization and interaction with others for personal growth and development. In different situations, returning to school in a dream can symbolize a longing for success or structure, the sensation of being evaluated, or the necessity to address a past trauma from your earlier days.

- **Roads in Dreams**

The mind's patterns of applying metaphors and meanings can be easily observed in the case of roads. A dream road symbolizes the voyage of life, encompassing the decisions we make, the challenges we face, and the possibilities that lie ahead. Take note of the road's condition and surroundings in your dream, including its width, length, smoothness, and overall environment. This can add depth to the interpretation of your dream.

- **Dreaming About Acquaintances**

Considering the possibility of dreaming about someone you haven't seen or thought of in years, it could potentially be interpreted as a message related to a specific time and place. When a friend from school appears in your dream, it's possible that something from that time in your life holds significance for the challenges you're facing now.

Examine the significance of that friend in your life. Summarize them in three words. Consider whether your friend's carefree, risk-taking, and fun-loving nature has influenced your recent experiences, and whether you could have potentially benefited from embracing these traits. Our connections with our friends provide valuable insights into our own identities, and this extends to their appearances in our dreams.

- **Dreams About Gifts**

Dreams about gifts can serve as a gentle reminder to the dreamer that they possess unique talents and abilities that they should wholeheartedly embrace. When presenting a gift to someone in a dream, it could indicate that you believe you possess something valuable to offer that individual in your everyday life. The recipient's reaction will provide insight into the expected response. When the gift is meticulously packaged, it gives the impression that a significant amount of effort has been invested in it. Do you have a specific aspect of your life that feels meticulously designed?

- **Bridges in Dreams**

Structures that connect two points, such as bridges, play a crucial role in transportation and infrastructure. They provide a means for people and vehicles to cross over obstacles such as rivers, valleys, or highways. Bridges are designed with careful consideration of various factors

Bridges can have a multitude of interpretations. For instance, at a fundamental level, a bridge serves as a means of crossing a gap or obstacle, symbolizing our transition from one thing to another. If our bridge is stable and solid, it suggests that the movements we are experiencing in our waking life are secure.

On the other hand, our dream bridge might be unstable and uncertain, suggesting some concerns about our present path in life. Do you have any bridges that require repair in your daily life? Take a careful look at your dream and you might find some hints about relationships that require your attention.

Perhaps you are attempting to reconcile a divide in a relationship in your current reality. Maybe you're starting to see a link with someone you've had different opinions with in the past.

A bridge over water can symbolize the importance of leaving the past behind and focusing on the future, similar to the saying "water under the bridge".

- **Sexual Dreams**

Sexual dreams often represent a deep longing for intimacy, connection, and physical closeness. On the other hand, sex in dreams can also symbolize the merging of your masculine and feminine archetypes (the anima and the animus, as described by Jung) or the importance of finding a harmonious balance between them. At times, dream sex may indicate a longing for authority, influence, or mastery over someone or something. On the whole, sex in dreams can be a symbol that is intricate and has many different aspects.

- **Dreams about Famous individuals**

Dreams about meeting celebrities often indicate a longing for fame and acknowledgment in one's daily life. Consider reflecting on your desire for increased recognition when you dream of a celebrity. Do you feel like your abilities are being overlooked? Have you ever desired to possess the same level of fame and fortune as this individual? Are you frustrated by the feeling that your dreams and goals are always just out of reach?

People are fascinated by celebrities because of the extraordinary experiences they have had, which many of us aspire to have in our own lives. Dreams about famous people often stem from a deep desire to personally encounter them. Meeting a celebrity in our dreams can be seen as a way for our dreams to fulfill our deepest desires.

- **Dreaming about Darkness**

The presence of darkness, symbolizing the absence of light, could suggest that the dreamer is going through a somber and weighty emotional state. If this is the situation, the dreamer should look for individuals or pursuits that illuminate their daily existence. On the other hand, their mood may be stable, but they may feel uncertain about a certain aspect of their daily life.

You may find it challenging to establish good relationships with your colleagues and feel like you are not being kept informed about routine office events. Maybe you sense a lack of clarity in your romantic relationship, unsure of which path to follow or where you stand with your partner. Examine the dream for any hints that may shed light on the specific aspect of your daily life it symbolizes. If the dream occurs in your school or university, it may symbolize your concern regarding the new material you are acquiring.

- **Dreams About Falling**

It is quite common to experience falling dreams, which are typically unpleasant. It is possible that a dream about falling indicates a sense of lacking support or experiencing a situation that makes you feel out of control in your waking life. From a certain perspective, a falling dream can be seen as the opposite of a flying dream, indicating that the events in your conscious life might be heading in an unfavorable direction. Take a moment to observe your surroundings in your dream. Do you notice any signs of descending into something? If you find yourself in a situation where you are repeatedly falling into a pile of desks, it may be worth considering if this is related to your work. When someone finds themselves descending onto a cluster of companions, it's possible that they may perceive a decline in their standing within their social circle. If the feeling of falling in the dream is enjoyable, it could indicate that things in your waking life are aligning perfectly.

- **Dreams About Graves**

Picture this: in your dream, a couple is strolling through a cemetery. As they go by a gravestone, the dreamer notices that her husband's name is carved into it. She is startled awake by the dream. Seeing a grave in a dream is often a metaphor for letting go of something, whether it's a relationship, a belief system, a life path, or even one's childhood. All the feelings that come with change in real life might find their way into them, including love, sadness, enthusiasm, loss, and fear. What have you buried? Think about it if you dream about a grave. Is it a sign that you should revive this long-dead treasure or that your life has improved since its burial?

- **Paralysis Dreams**

Paralysis dreams sometimes involve the dreamer attempting to flee from an assailant but finding that their legs are immobile. On the other hand, you could discover that you are entirely paralyzed when you attempt to rise from a chair. Even though these nightmares are real, they might be related to the physiological dream state in which our brain tells our spinal cord neurons to turn off. Because of this, we are unable to act out our dreams and experience a brief paralysis.

Perhaps the real physiological paralysis that goes along with dreaming sleep happens in the dream itself when we imagine ourselves paralyzed.

Symbolically, paralysis in a dream could represent a state of being unable to move or escape from a problem. Such dreams are common among depressed people. The same holds true for people whose emotions, like grief, prevent them from moving.

- **Planes**

Getting aboard an aircraft could be a sign that you're about to start a new chapter in your waking life, whether it's a major undertaking, a journey, or a change in perspective. It could be a sign that you're feeling a bit "bored" with your current waking life endeavors if all you can think about is getting on board.

Planes symbolize travel since they transport us from one location to another. Plane rides, being lengthier than road trips, are often symbolic of the more substantial life journeys we're on. If the journey is fraught with danger, it could be because you are experiencing "turbulent" times in your life right now. Things may be going swimmingly in your life if you're having a pleasant and uneventful trip.

Maybe you feel like you're facing a lot of problems in your daily life if you're having trouble getting to the airline on time. Another interpretation is that you aren't ready to embark on a new adventure because you can't find your plane ticket.

- **Detention center or Prison**

Inmates face punishment, confinement, and the loss of their freedom in a prison. Are you ever feeling stifled by anything going on in your life? Is there anything that makes you feel like you're being punished? Maybe you think you're deserving of your ideal prison if you're a prisoner in real life. Consider how these emotions compare to the ones you experience on a regular basis.

Does the prison have any additional inmates? Maybe that individual stands for a part of yourself that you try to keep hidden. You can be shackled by outdated ideas and standards that are holding you back from moving forward. Maybe you're in a relationship or at work where you can't really be yourself. Maybe when you're awake, you don't feel very free. Somebody might be trying to stop you.

Would you rather do the term in prison or try to get out? How you handle the problem might be comparable to this.

- **Dreams About Shoulders**

Having a dream about a certain area of your body is common and often symbolic. Perhaps you feel as though someone or something is sneaking up on you if you dream that you are peeking over your shoulder. Something or someone from your history can be symbolized by this.

As in taking a problem upon one's shoulders or being there for someone when they're down and out, shoulders can also mean duties and loads. Your dream about leaning on someone's shoulder could be a message that you need their support or that you're putting a burden on them. You can decipher the gesture's significance based on your emotional state in the dream.

Perhaps the dream is trying to inform you that you're holding the world's problems in your hands.

- **Reptiles and Insects**

For a lot of people, spiders are the very definition of eerie and terrifying. When you dream about spiders, they can be a symbol of your real-life fears. For example, if you dream that spiders are scurrying over your textbooks, it could be a sign that you're feeling particularly anxious about your present course of study.

Or maybe you're fascinated by the spider in your dream. How enchanted were you by the intricate web your dream spider spun? Perhaps something in your waking life is symbolizing this dream's web of curiosity and wonder.

Dreams involving snakes are not uncommon. The ancient people looked to them as a sign of healing and change because of their reputation for shedding skins. Are you going through a period of healing or loss? Also, snakes can stand in for anything you're afraid of.

After giving in to the serpent's temptation in Eden's Garden, Adam and Eve were both punished for their transgression. Some people associate snakes with negative emotions like guilt, humiliation, retribution, or temptation. The conflict in your dream could be a metaphor for a real war you've witnessed in the news or a personal struggle you're facing at home, in your relationships, at work, or in your studies. Am I to understand that you are currently engaged in a struggle? Do you have mixed feelings about any part of who you are?

- **Battle**

Dreaming about a battle could be a sign that you need to resolve an issue in your waking life. Perhaps the dream itself will provide you with information that will help you resolve the conflict. When you dream about surrendering instead of fighting in a war, it could be a message from your dream world to think about finding a peaceful resolution to this dispute in real life. Dreams about battle might sometimes serve as health warnings. Sometimes, even before you feel any symptoms, your unconscious mind may have already registered an impending illness, and your dreams may have begun to "battle" against it.

- **Dreams About Abduction**

The interpretation of a dream involving kidnapping can vary depending on the specific events that occurred within the dream. Dreams about kidnapping often suggest a sense of vulnerability or lack of control in one's daily life. Feeling trapped in a certain situation could be represented by an unhealthy relationship or a stressful job.

It is possible that this dream suggests a lack of personal autonomy, with someone else exerting control over your life, particularly if that person assumes the role of the "kidnapper" in the dream.

Dreams about kidnapping can also indicate a sense of being inundated with responsibilities or obligations. It is possible that the dream signifies a desire to reclaim control and independence from the pressures imposed on you in your daily life. It may also indicate the necessity of distancing yourself from detrimental influences or circumstances that are impeding your progress.

- **Dreams about toilets**

A toilet located near the house holds significant symbolism in dream interpretations, often associated with financial matters. A toilet in a restroom can be seen as a symbol of prosperity. In the dream, if you find yourself in a situation where others can observe you while using the toilet, it may suggest that there is a source of stress in your life. Consider the scenario where the toilet is located in a public place rather than your home. This situation may prompt you to reflect on the concept of freedom and how you express your emotions in your daily life.

The dream itself may indicate that there is an attempt to evade challenging and conflicting circumstances, either by you or someone else. If there are other individuals using a public toilet or restroom without proper attire, it may indicate a desire for privacy in such situations. Dreaming about a toilet without doors suggests a lack of control and reliance on others. Dreaming about other people utilizing a public restroom while being exposed can serve as a reminder of the importance of personal privacy and self-preservation. Dreaming of a malfunctioning toilet suggests that unexpected resources may manifest themselves.

CHAPTER FIVE

Using Dreams for Emotional Healing

Dreams can be an effective tool for emotional healing, giving a secure environment in which to process unresolved emotions and prior traumas. Identify and understand emotional elements in your dreams. Pay attention to reoccurring feelings and how they affect your daily life.

Dream Reentry: Dream Reentry is a technique in which you re-enter a dream (by visualization or lucid dreaming) to address and overcome emotional concerns.

Dream Dialogue: Have a conversation with dream figures or symbols to discover their messages and release pent-up emotions.

Therapeutic Dream Writing: Write down your dreams and consider their emotional meaning. This technique can help you develop clarity and insight into your emotions.

Nightmare Resolution: Discover ways for transforming and resolving dreams, which frequently contain intense emotional content relating to fear, trauma, or anxiety.

Problem Solving and Creativity

Dreams can inspire creativity and generate novel answers to issues.

Incubating Dreams: Before going to bed, set a clear objective or focus on a specific problem to encourage your subconscious to work on it while you sleep.

Lucid Dreaming and Creativity: Use lucid dreaming to actively investigate creative concepts or scenarios. Visualization and dream control are two ways that can help you improve your creativity.

Recording and Reflecting: Keep a dream journal to record and reflect on creative insights and problem-solving ideas that arise during your dreams.

Symbolic Solutions: Learn how to interpret dream symbols, which may provide metaphorical solutions or new views on real-life difficulties.

Personal Development and Self-discovery

Dreams reflect our inner selves, providing significant insights for personal development and self-discovery.

Self-reflection: Examine your dreams to find trends, behaviors, and attitudes that may require attention or modification. Consider how these insights can help you in your own progress.

Archetypal Exploration: Explore Jungian archetypes in your dreams to gain insight into many elements of your personality and mind. Recognize how these archetypes shape your behavior and decisions.

Life Transitions: Dreams can help you handle big life transitions including work shifts, relationships, and personal milestones. Dreams can bring advice and comfort during times of transition.

Goal Setting: Determine and establish personal goals based on the lessons received from your dreams. Make a plan to achieve these objectives, drawing inspiration and guidance from your dreams.

Interpreting Personal Dreams

Interpreting your unique dreams can provide great insights and wisdom. Practical guidelines for efficient dream interpretation include:

Keeping a Dream Journal: Record your dreams on a regular basis, noting elements like feelings, symbols, and events. Examine and analyze your entries to discover patterns and repeating topics.

Identifying key symbols: Concentrate on the most important symbols in your dreams and investigate their particular meaning. Consider how these symbols correspond to your waking experiences and feelings.

Contextual Analysis: Examine the environment, characters, and plot. Consider how these elements interact and what they might symbolize.

Emotional Resonance: Pay attention to the emotions you felt in the dream and how they relate to your current emotional state. Emotions might reveal vital information about the dream's meaning.

Seeking Feedback: Share your dreams with trustworthy friends, family, or a therapist to receive new perspectives and insights. Collaborative interpretation can reveal additional levels of significance.

Integrating Insights: Apply the insights learned from dream interpretation to your daily life. Utilize these revelations to effect good change, solve issues, and further your own development.

You can tap into a wealth of wisdom and potential within yourself by utilizing the power of dreams for emotional healing, problem solving, creativity, personal development, and self-discovery. Personal dream interpretation is a transforming technique that can help you gain a better understanding of yourself and live a more fulfilling life.

END

www.ingramcontent.com/pod-product-compliance
Lightning Source LLC
Chambersburg PA
CBHW051817250726
48659CB00005B/1536